ALSO BY PETER DAVIS

Hitler's Mustache (Barnwood, 2006)
Poetry! Poetry! Poetry! (Bloof, 2010)

PETER DAVIS

BLOOF BOOKS

9	Making Out		
11	A Note to Tina		
12	The Interesting Thing about Gloves		
13	The Mustaches of the Past		
14	An Explanation		
15	Tuesday Evening with Tina		
16	One Tina Note		
17	The People in the Middle	I'm a Person, Tina	29
18	Options	Seriously, Tina	30
19	The Alsoness of Living	My Education	31
20	Old Problems	Skateboarding	32
21	I Am a Failure, Tina	The Package	33
23	The Truth	The Is a Crack in the Windshield	35
24	Through the Blinds, as I'm Peeing, I Can See Tina in the Moon	A Letter from the Past	36
		How Today Becomes a Creepy Spider	37
25	The Stairs	A Sonnet for Tina	38
26	Memories	Sylvia Plath	39
27	The People That Exist	Emily Dickinson	40
		Poser	41
		Certain Things People Do	42
		Situations and the Nature of the Situation	43
		Nature and the Nature of the Nature	44
		I Am Not a Failure, Tina	45
		How It Happens	46
		Better Person	47

Copyright © 2013 by PETER DAVIS • All rights reserved. • ISBN-13: 978-0-9826587-3-4

48	A Note about Orange		
49	Not Exactly What I Mean		
50	The Facts		
51	My Brother	Crime, Tina	67
53	Wake Up, Tina	The Government	68
54	A Warning	Crazy	69
55	How Something Isn't New	Sleeping in a Tree with Tina	70
56	Professional Depression	Around in the Area	71
57	Obviousness	Instructions on How to Palpitate Best	72
58	Eddie Van Halen	So Long	73
59	Loving the Affected	Mother's Day	75
60	The Boxed	Having Real Ideas	76
61	Form	The Spirit World	77
62	Meeting Arrangements	According to All the Dead People	78
63	In a Traffic Jam with Tina	One Problem with Children	79
64	Tina, Because I'm Lazy	Realer	80
65	8:51 in the Evening	The Rescue Operation	81
		Hurts	82
		The Situation Often Referred to as Poetry	83
		I Said Goodbye	84
		The Egyptian Revolution of 2011	85

Acknowledgments **88**

About the Author **89**

Bloof Books, Central New Jersey • www.bloofbooks.com

So what do you say? That I invented the beautiful name of Laura to give myself something to talk about and to engage many to talk about me! And that in fact there is no Laura in my mind except the poetic Laurel for which I evidently have aspired with long-continued unwearying zeal; and that concerning the living Laura, by whose person I seem to be captured, everything is manufactured; that my poems are fictitious, my sighs pretended. Well, on this head I wish it were all a joke, that it were a pretense and not a madness!

—Petrarch, *Epistolae Familiares*

We loved each other with a premature love, marked by a fierceness that so often destroys adult lives.

—Vladimir Nabokov, *Lolita*

Now it's over, I'm dead, and I haven't done anything that I want,
Or, I'm still alive and there's nothing I want to do.

—They Might Be Giants, "Dead"

MAKING OUT

First, Tina, there is some kind of talk
or isolation or something that brings
us together. Then, in some
moment, we kiss. This kiss leads to
more kissing. It is good to start french
kissing here. I mean, moving our tongues
against the other's and having
these wide, gaping mouths.
Sometimes, when we take a break
from kissing, you might even wipe
your mouth with your shirtsleeve.
If I am lucky and there is enough time
I will very slowly begin touching
your waist and very slowly start
working my hand under your shirt
and moving it up toward your shoulders.
When I reach your bra, I will feel
humbled and in awe so I will feel
your bra some. Then I will back my hand down
a little and come up again, this
time trying to wedge my fingers
between your bra and your skin. Tina,
we will be french kissing this whole time.
If I am lucky I will soon feel your
nipple. I will have to use the back
of my hand, wedged under the underwire,

to push up and give my fingers a few
small inches to move. Hopefully one of us
will unsnap your bra. Bras that unsnap
in front are easier to deal with. For this
reason, they are very sexy.
This will really be something.
After a bit, I will slowly slide my
hand down from your breasts and
begin to dig between the waist
of your pants and your skin. If it is
a tight squeeze, the best thing possible
would be for you to just unbutton
your pants and even lower your zipper.
Otherwise, I will unbutton your pants.
This is very exciting. I will move my
hand even lower until I reach
the top of your underwear. I will rub
all around the area above your
underwear. I will begin to rub
your underwear. Then I will
try to get my fingers between your skin
and your underwear. I will be
successful or you will adjust
position or something else
will just happen, Tina.

A NOTE TO TINA

No matter what anyone says,
you've got a beautiful way about you that
suggests something more, better
than regular grammar. I was thinking
of assailing you with metaphorical examples
but instead decided on nothing. Thus,
we find ourselves in the midst of this,
perhaps bored or stunned dumb.
There is no other way of displaying this
to the world, but, believe me,
if I could make a billboard I would.
I would put it on your highway.
You would drive by and say, Ah.
It's like a Poison album, but different.

THE INTERESTING THING ABOUT GLOVES

The interesting thing about gloves
is how they provide a layer, a boundary,
a fence (if you will) between the weird yard of your
skin and the weird yard of the thing you're touching.
Often, on lab days, when no one's around and
the secretaries are at lunch, I will open the scroll
that reads like a menu of torture methods. I always
stop about midway through, fatigue mounting
me into a prison bitch. Lazing on the sofa,
dreaming of the time change, dreaming of the Jedi,
dreaming of the weird dreams of sleepwalk. Still,
to relieve the pressure, I'm going to have to
move quicker than I am accustomed to. I am used
to being very slow and snailish. I'm usually
proud of my sloth, but these days, Tina,
I find my normally stable brain
is teetering and then, like a tiny bird egg, I'm somehow
lost in the grass, the perfect vegetable for a snake.

THE MUSTACHES OF THE PAST

It is true, Tina,
that some men in the past
sported enormous mustaches.
Some of them
(even the grotesquely deformed)
grew mustaches like
cranes lifting and lowering the
mandible. In some cases
scholars no bigger than a thumb
measured the mustaches
and deemed them exceedingly
woolly. "It is like a world of pubic
hair," said one. Another said,
"These mustaches are a dense
legal system through which there
are many courts of appeal."

AN EXPLANATION

You're a silly girl most of the time,
and when you're not being
silly you act like
a kid which is mostly beautiful
but sometimes
inconvenient. That's the thing
about kids, Tina. They're
inconvenient.
They are inconvenient, Tina.
Say you have something
you want to do or you want
to go get something or just
watch some TV or something.
Kids always screw that
stuff up. You've got to *know* that,
Tina! You've just got to!

TUESDAY EVENING WITH TINA

Most of my life I've been very confused. The amount of time that
I've spent confused is equal to the cold strangeness of hunting
very small animals. I know most of us know what I mean.
We know the feeling of stalking through a field
in an olive green hunting cap, with rust-colored boots, and
flannel trim on our gloves. We all know the buttery rush of memory
and the half second of Death springing into the wounded torso
of some furry little situation of small animalness.
Who has not yelled to the gods? Who hasn't screamed to a million
unseen fences and tossed rings over hundreds of human heads?
Everyone has these same messy nightmares.
I'm of the type who is confused and messy.
All some small animal situation myself. You know how
this goes back. Before long you're consulting your mother
about your uncle who is a tall gentleman with a wide, brown mustache.
It gets gone almost before you even get there. It's like you
wouldn't notice but you do. In that position, you wake, put on your
clothes and reach into open air. By constantly changing the
empty space around you, you feel like a rich man for microseconds,
and that's good enough, sort of.

ONE TINA NOTE

I might repair a small
hole in the foundation
of my house.
I may create a bee repellent or
some brutal bug zapper.
The possibilities aren't staggering
but they're impressive
in their way. The greatest thing
might be a sort of paper hat
that is folded so as to
frame the face effectively.
With my round face, I need
something angular,
while you, with your whatever face,
need whatever you need in the way
of paper hats.

THE PEOPLE IN THE MIDDLE

The people in
the middle
are waist-like
and also similar to
a belt.
The belt shape,
or the oval,
or semicircle,
is ubiquitous everywhere
you roll, Tina.
Say you are in
a motorcycle gang
and have a certain
patch sewn
to your black jacket.
This sort of thing
is predictable.
Please, try
to calm down,
Tina.
Jesus!
You're totally
overreacting by,
like,
freaking out!

OPTIONS

I never know if the mail I receive is really for me. Sure, some of it is signed, "love, Mom" and some of it personally addresses me with salutations like "Hey Kyle" or "Dear Kyle" or, even, "For my beloved, Kyle," but mostly it's all pretty ambiguous. The mail carrier won't look me in the face and when I call out to her, in a good natured way, like, say, "Excuse me, Ms. I think you dropped an envelope," she never responds with anything but a purple glare. I should say too that that shade of purple is not meant for a face. What confuses me most are the addresses, which rarely actually indicate the street I live on. I live on Grant Street, but most of my mail says stuff like "Grum Street" and "Grime Stipe" and "Gutter Humper." The zip code is rarely correct and many of the actual packages I receive are clearly meant for others because they'll say things like "Dear Margery" and "Hello Sven" and "Good Evening Mrs. Turnbuckle." Still, this stuff winds up in my hands and I'm left to consider the possibility that these are for me, that I might be Sven and live on Grum Street. But, here's the thing, I know I'm not Mrs. Turnbuckle and, even if I was, I wouldn't open her mail.

THE ALSONESS OF LIVING

Other interesting things include certain branches of science and different pastry shops. I also am a fan of zero-calorie flavored waters that usually come in plastic bottles. Some people really like saunas. The world can be like that. I've noticed that some men enjoy wearing gold, silver, or platinum bracelets! It takes time to notice, but as the weather changes during the course of a day, the temperature may vary slightly, or drastically. This type of circumstance can be appreciated for what it is. I enjoy wearing shoes, but some people don't like them. Once, it occurred to me that people have various thoughts regarding sex and that one person may personally really enjoy a certain sexual idea that another person may enjoy too, but to a lesser degree. I find the whole event of being a person is a tad bizarre. Just today, returning from an errand in my car, I noticed there were other people out there and that, by and large, they look different from one another! Everywhere I seemed to look, there was a person and that person was different in appearance from the previous person! Wild! Coming into my house I noticed the evidence of animals, perhaps birds or chipmunks. I thought, there are bats hiding in dark places right now. As I understand it, other people have thoughts as well. Even Tina. Some may have seen the evidence of animals too!

OLD PROBLEMS

My wife calls on the phone and I answer it. Have you
received phone calls before, Tina? Do you know what
this is like? Well, then why don't you keep your
mouth shut for a change. The phone
is this device that allows one human (or a group of humans)
to communicate with another human (or a group of humans).
You hold it against the side of your head. Imagine
that it's a banana and you put one end near your mouth
and the other end near your ear. When you speak, the other
person (who could be as close, say, as a near neighbor, or
as far away, say, as all the way around the earth), who is
also holding a "phone," can hear what you say and when
that person speaks you can hear it on your "end of the line,"
on your "phone." My wife calls and she's lonely so she's
calling me to say so. I respond to her with some sort of
reassuring statement, like, glad you called. This kind
of banter continues for a few minutes and then it's
over with, I'm back to being off the phone and back to
helping you with all your dumbfuck ideas. So cool it.
Just take a step back and put the ABBA record down.

I AM A FAILURE, TINA

When watching TV, when watching a DVD, when listening to a CD,
when carefully considering questions of religion and philosophy,
I am a failure.
The mirror always sees failure.
Petting a dog or rubbing her behind her ears, I fail badly.
When I whistle, I fail as a whistler.
Taking an elevator, escalator, or bus, my failure is obvious.
When eating candy and cake and ice cream, I am a dessert failure.
Remembering happy moments from elementary school, I am failing.
This failing comes easy.
It actually feels good because it's so easy.
I was touching another human's cheek, in a tender manner, and I was failing.
I was stating that I was a failure, failing.
When I was failing, I was a failure.
When I was considering the cartoon? Failing.
Holding a bottle? Failing.
Wearing my glasses? Really failing.
Walking through the grass is a type of failure.
Changing my clothes I really feel like a failure.
The way I fail at each spectacular moment is breathtaking. I look at these
    moments in a failing way.
I love them in a failing manner.
Using a hammer or an electric drill.
Reading a newspaper.
When I take a bath in my kids' bath water, I don't get as clean as I could.
    I am a hygienic failure.

I am really failurish.

When I find certain definitions, I am failing in a dictionary sort of way.

All this failure is moving along as planned.

The failure is written into the text.

I am trying to change this sense of failure, but I am

not having much success.

I feel like a failure often.

Sometimes, even all alone with my thoughts, I feel like a failure.

No matter how many failures I don't have, or have,

I am a failure.

If I have some success, I am still a failure.

If I am told that I am not a failure, I am still a failure.

I am always failing because I cannot succeed.

I can succeed and still I fail.

I can win the race and still fail.

I am a failure regardless of what place I get.

I am a failure in every race.

When I sleep at night, I sleep as a failure.

Even if magazines and television programs proclaim

me a success, I am a failure.

When I achieve something, I have failed.

When I accomplish a goal, I fail.

THE TRUTH

The beard, Tina!
The beard is, in fact, growing!
It is growing!
This is an indication of
microscopic vibration.
But it is the beard I wish to welcome!
Yes, in another lifetime I was in love with you!
Yes, I found you very attractive!
You, arriving on a slow, heavy bus!
What is important about you
is impossible to identify
but I'm going to visit a psychiatrist.
I believe a combination of
counseling and medication will distill
the beard into meaning!
I might also further my education!
I may incur debt that I'm willing
to pay off!

THROUGH THE BLINDS, AS I'M PEEING, I CAN SEE TINA IN THE MOON

The whole way to the
approximate "night hour" is difficult.
I see small bats of light
ricocheting in a box and
signaling some cipher. I need
a U-boat codebreaker.
I need a generalized theory
to brace this shoddy shit.
I am thinking of a number from
1 to 100, though it is
Egyptian, or something, that
doesn't, like,
make sense to you.
What am I trying to say?
I was getting to that?
I'm fingering a question mark.
I know what the girls from
my middle school felt like.
I mean, I had some knowledge.

THE STAIRS

The stairs were constructed in such a way
so as to emphasize the difference in height
between each individual platform. I was thinking
about that when I found myself face to face
with Tina. She was holding a jar.
I felt my inside body begin to levitate through
my outside body. I was, like, "Tina!" And
she was, like, nothing, and just stood there
all stone-faced and empty looking. At the table,
her parents sat lonely, with wet, begging
eyes. In a way, it was all sorta stupid.
I remember saying to Tina (and I'm saying this to you
now only because I know she'll probably say
something) but I was, like, "Tina, please, put your
tape recorder away and just enjoy this!"

MEMORIES

Your gymnastics coach was inconsolable.
I remember how you teased your hair
and dabbed your eyelid. Your poor blue
eyelid, all fluorescent with the valley of the shadow.
Your little fish belly eyelids weren't alit
for no reason. I remember times
when you seemed like a robot, all stiff
with certain noticeable side effects.
Come on, Tina!
You know how to fold a tablecloth, Tina.
Don't give me any crap!
You know how to fold a tablecloth, Tina.

THE PEOPLE THAT EXIST

A person has a car, Tina, and they use it to drive places.
A person has a voice and so they use it, they
sing or talk or grunt in funny, greasy ways.
People use their mouths to maul
their food, or to kiss a loved one.
People have friends. They call friends and say words.
They exchange glances and noises.
One person buys another person dinner!
One person has an idea and they ask another person
for an opinion!
Life is always moving into a new event.
Have you witnessed the nature of popular movies and
the always-changing-into-something-that-is-the-sameness
of pop music? You are probably aware of the passage
of time and the little anomalies?
That's not the sort of thing I'm thinking about in
this particular event. Here, I'm addressing
something both more primitive and
stranger. To me, there is such a thing as a swimming pool
that swims in you.
Imagine the way neighbors have to negotiate the fence
between their properties. Do you see where I'm going?
In spite of everything, it's tiring using
language to get to something.
Certain people have certain strengths and certain weaknesses.
All of this stuff comes to light sometimes.

Or it doesn't. Who knows?

People know about mysteries or they don't.

People understand mysteries or they don't.

A person can look at a cloud and see a shape, or not.

I'M A PERSON, TINA

"Victorious homecoming" and
"winning one the right way" is really
nice, especially if you
"would want your son to be like this" and
even if you want to
(something else).
The "fans who insisted" on being
part of the television set
are beautiful in their "this is great
for the city" way.
"You can bet this city will be
lit up blue."
Even Peyton's wife Ashley
believes they "did such a great job
this year and it's so exciting."

SERIOUSLY, TINA

It's a football game and it's important
that one team beats the other team.
I don't care whether you understand.
Get over yourself, Tina!
All these years, with your fucking friends,
and your exaggerated sense of self!
I don't know how your Schwan Man tolerated you!
I've met a ton of record store employees
and you're not even wearing denim!
Sure, all of us make errors,
but the way you prance around here is ridiculous.
Seriously, Tina, grow up! We're all
tired of your histrionics!

MY EDUCATION

There's high school and then
there's college. I say, college was
okay, but let's go back to high
school. And I don't even know
that high school is better than
college, I'm just saying. I mean,
I went to college and even
got a master's degree (twice)
but I never really appreciated
the world unveiled to me.
I appreciate the veil, Tina. I like
high school where you know
everyone and have kissed
a higher percentage of your
graduating class. I got even
more play in middle school.
That's when french kissing
was like finding a cool place
to skate. By *skate* I mean
skateboard. Which is what
I'm talking about, you
fucking dorky bitch.

SKATEBOARDING

I skate for me and my homeboys!
We grind and carve!
Let's skate! We yell that shit, Tina.
We fucking yell it!
We're behind the grocery store, Tina,
shredding this curb and
John Law comes up and is like
Scram! Fuckers! So lame!
And I'm adjusting my beret.
And Tina, my skate Betty, I know you
love me, but I can't
even explain how much
I will skate or die!

THE PACKAGE

First, there was the cardboard box
that was wrapped in clear tape.
I got a knife. Then there was a box wrapped
in sticky paper. Then another layer of sticky paper.
Then another layer. Then there was a layer
of clear tape. Then, another box. When I
opened this box, there was a jar wrapped
in sticky paper and more clear tape. There
were a bunch of layers of each. It was hard
work. I was starting to sweat. When I finally got
to the jar, the lid was glued shut. It took me
a while to dislodge it. The jar was filled with glue,
but deep in the center of the glue was a small
package wrapped in clear tape. Below those
layers of clear tape, was a sort of tiny tarp
that seemed plastered to a layer of tape beneath it.
I peeled the tape and the tarp. I cut
through the layer beneath that.
There was a box rife with screws. It was
very screwy. I undid the screws I could undo and
got a small hacksaw for some of the others. I
was laughing a little to myself by now. Also,
I was frustrated. I had broken one of my fingernails.
Beneath the screwy box was a ball of tape
wrapped with sticky paper and a hard shell
like thing coated with a bony chocolate.

It was late by now. I chiseled the shell and fought
my way through the tape and sticky paper.
It was a loosening situation. There was much
pulling and slackening. Through it all, not
a single phone call, Tina. And that's what I think about
now, Tina. Not a single fucking phone call.

THERE IS A CRACK IN THE WINDSHIELD

Friends make agreements,
they break agreements,
they make new agreements.
I'm aware of all this, Tina.
Over beer,
over a shot,
over a covered bridge.
You may be experiencing a decent
ride through the country.
Bummer there is no super
car that carries us.
I can hear boards rattling.
Not that I know anything about
rattling boards, but remember
I am writing words.
You've got an idea, Tina?
Me too. When the rain slowly starts
it takes a couple of minutes
for the wipers to go on.

A LETTER FROM THE PAST

It is not good news to get bad news, especially
involving words like "degenerative" and "chronic"
and "analogy." You have to adjust your ears in such
a situation, so as to loosen the vibrations a bit,
and allow them to trickle toward your innards.
My innards are powerful lonely and my teardrops
contain a little jewel of the past. To imagine
the decisions of childhood matter! That there
was never any house money! O, Tina, I wish
I was a new culprit of dawn! I wish I could dredge
the dregs from this soupy mess. As a kid you have
eyes that you use to imagine and as an adult
you have eyes that you use to reimagine. The
pattern isn't perfect, but it's close enough to
remind you of home. And where is a home for
someone from the future? In your bones, idiot!
In the way they hold themselves in your body.

HOW TODAY BECOMES A CREEPY SPIDER

You have hopes, maybe.
Maybe, you have financial problems
or thoughts like lasers. Scattered thoughts
like scattered lasers. You may imagine
a laser shooting through a prism.
You imagine the prism jiggling.
Prism Jiggling.
Their first record,
Thoughts like Lasers, Lasers like BBs on a Tiled Floor,
rocks.
Tina, after a while, you cut your hair.
Then, you notice bits of hair in the bathwater.
It is now beginning.
In the background, the TV says,
"puberty isn't for kids anymore."

A SONNET FOR TINA

Well I wonder how it happens that the weather
where you are isn't exactly the same as the weather
where I am. I'm no meteorologist, but it just seems logical
that the weather would be exactly the same everywhere
and yet, here we are: you in a very warm
climate, me where it is brisker. I also find it interesting
that not every single human being agrees completely
with all other human beings. In short, people have
slight variations, which seems unlikely, to say the least,
and yet, again, we find ourselves surrounded with
certain evidence. I don't know about you, but I used
to enjoy crime dramas. Also, I've played Frisbee and
ridden a go-cart a little as a child. It's starting to
come together I think. This mystery about the weather.

SYLVIA PLATH

It is this darkness in me that
rowboats out from shore, saying
"What the fuck?" to more darkness,
like people discovering sex. They
all think, "Well, this is nice."
Why shouldn't they?
They sneak up like mountains
and build new children's hospitals.
Oh, back there I am
sick.
I am way back there crinkled
in a blanket. The way
eyes move freaks me out.
I'm, like, crazy.

EMILY DICKINSON

She's all, like, "I like writing" and
"I'm good at it." She's, like,
"I like white and looking out
of windows," and, like, "I like
baking bread and the Bible," and, like,
"I like my alone time."
She's like, "It's cool."
They're like, "I don't know if it's cool."
She's like, "It is."
They're like, "You're weird."
And she's like, "No, I'm not. Maybe
you're weird."
And they're like, "No, you're weird."
And she's like, "Am not."
And they're like, "Are too."
And she's like, "na-uh.""
And they're like, "uh-huh."
And she's like "Whatever!"
And "Talk to the hand!" And
"Whatever." And
they're like "Whatever."
and she's like, "Whatever."

POSER

When the snow really
falls, one can produce
snow forts, all gutted
from giant snow piles.
If one is not a giant pile
of snow, one doesn't
have to watch *Cocktail*
on TV. But not doing so
would be pretty stupid
and pretty immature.
Besides, as a biologist,
I have obligations
to science that don't allow
me to change sides!
Freedom isn't free, Tina!

CERTAIN THINGS PEOPLE DO

I understand that people
murder each other and
lift weights obsessively,
tanning and whatnot.
O, I don't know what else they do.
A lot.
Some people pose for photographs
holding giant wreaths and
other people sit in chairs
that are far too small for their
long, thin bodies.
Certain people have to make
important phone calls
and others curl their lips in funny ways.
I'm the sort of person
who gets depressed and then
feels like a little valve somewhere
is leaking. It's complicated.
I keep thinking of things, Tina.
I keep thinking of them.
Perhaps sometime you will have
to use the phrase "extra frames"
or "may worsen with."

SITUATIONS AND THE NATURE OF THE SITUATION

I had purchased a new proton accelerator
but Tina was angry, "Because," she said,
"there's nothing wrong with the old proton
accelerator." My son was upset because
he wanted an electron decelerator.
I screamed, "Listen, everyone," (we were all
crying and hugging) "I got a new proton
accelerator because we needed it."
Tina said again, "No, we didn't."
But I pointed out that the old proton accelerator
wasn't actually accelerating the protons, but
was simply exaggerating them. Tina got
a stunned look on her face.
"Oh," she said, "I didn't realize that."

NATURE AND THE NATURE OF THE NATURE

There was a Giant Spot of Nothing
in the cupboard that I wouldn't have noticed
except for the spotlight on it
and the disco music playing and the announcer
in my ear yelling, "Behold! Giant Spot
of Nothing! Behold! Giant Spot of Nothing! Bow down!"
So I beheld and I bowed.
And I began a fractured worship. I received
divine inspiration and wrote a holy book.
My book began, "In the beginning there was
a Giant Spot of Nothing in the cupboard
so shall it be in the middle and in the end, as well."
Nobody was interested in my new religion.
Seriously, Tina, the indifference was overwhelming.

I AM NOT A FAILURE, TINA

I am not a failure, but a human.
When I enjoy various aspects of humanity, I am not a failure.
Even if I don't enjoy various aspects of humanity, I am not a failure.
Or, I am a failure.
I can't quite know for sure.
I believe I am not a failure, but I'm only guessing.
When I notice how human I am standing, let's say, in front of a window
and catching a faint reflection in the glass, I also notice
my status as a failure or not a failure.
When I consider my status I often have second thoughts.
One thought: failure. Another thought: not a failure.
As a human, determined to stay so, I often don't consider
myself human. Instead, I look at myself as a graph or a record
for what might have been a human.
I am an inadequate but passable record-keeper.
As for records, I spin on a turntable in a failure-like way,
with the skipping and the warbling.
As for my non-failure, it is beautiful and not a failure.
It is very, very enjoyable. I like not failing.
I'm even a fan of positive reinforcement.

HOW IT HAPPENS

When I settle into myself
it's like a piano, or at least
the keys being pushed
(like something).
There is the volume control
for the TV and the hat
that is static.
This static hat sits here and then
shuffles away, leaving little
dung.
Hung in the hall, on hooks of
gold, hardly dripping
any sweat, I see the prisoners
that I wasn't even thinking about.
I'm not even thinking about
them now, instead
I'm concentrating on
a bullet that isn't acting like a
bullet. No, it's a mullet.
No, the word "poultry," or
"poetry." No, it's not even that.
I'm talking about sailing
science and wings
spread through the teeth
of a lisper. I mean, the wind.
No, Tina, I mean the
transparent fist.

BETTER PERSON

When at a restaurant, a person could always leave a larger tip
and I am certainly a person. Today, I saw a person flagrantly
litter and I did not get up and retrieve the litter, but I did condemn her
in my mind, thinking, I was better than she was. I could be a better
person than that. I should probably be more gracious
with my forgiveness and should probably be less
hopeful for apologies. I'm really awful on the whole.
I should probably purchase less gas, less energy, less water.
I should do so much less. I should do less so much more
often. It's impossible to catch the guy who is leading
this race. But I could try harder. That's what I'm doing, Tina.
Motherfuck! What do you think this is about?

A NOTE ABOUT ORANGE

Orange is not
a color you want
to get on your
bad side, Tina.
Orange is always
like "I'll fuck you up"
and "Bitch,
I'm gonna stick you."

NOT EXACTLY WHAT I MEAN

Tina, instead of "Happy Thanksgiving" you
should say something else.
I mention this only because I know
that saying "Happy Thanksgiving" is
like saying "Swim in pig blood" or
"Put guts in your boots." People who
say "Happy Thanksgiving" are often
people who approve of murder,
rape, and child molestation. Not all
of them are like this, but a huge
portion of them are.
I do not approve of those things.
That is why I'm saying you shouldn't
say "Happy Thanksgiving," Tina.
Saying "Happy Thanksgiving" is
like filling a person's nose with
locusts or stuffing onions in a dead
person's throat. Nobody wants that.
I'm a horrible person and even I don't
want that. Even if you like
gory stuff, you have to admit
that's some pretty bad shit.

THE FACTS

These are the facts, Tina.
Turkeys enjoy torture.
They are adept at waterboarding
and hooding, Tina. They are experts
at sleep deprivation and leaving
white lights on all the time.
Turkeys like attaching electric
batteries to people's genitalia.
Turkeys also like genocide.
If you are interested in genocide, Tina,
or torture, you should
become friends with a turkey
who will stay up late telling you
torture and genocide stories.
Turkeys like genocide because
they like exterminating entire groups
of people. They like how the mass
graves fill up with people and so
all the extra dirt has to go somewhere
and they always make a giant hill
so that in winter they have a good
place to go sledding. Also, they like
the smell of stuff burning. Tina, turkeys
feel like genocide brings them together.
They all feel more friendly and warmer
and TV shows get better because
everyone feels like family.

MY BROTHER

My brother rode whole teams of cougars through
the mall, screaming, his long blond hair ribboning out
behind him, his legs hairy and ribs hard
as asphalt. When he drank, he held jugs of water
before himself and let himself pour the water
into himself before himself would devour loaves
of bread and so many biscuits that, though the bakery
held 1,600 bakers (there were two dozen workers involved
in the washing of bakers' hats alone), there was a break room
filled with message therapists. There were days no one
slept more than a couple of hours at a time. My
brother would eat for weeks, but when it was time for
battle he'd eat less. He'd still eat, but they'd close
the third shift. Some bakers missed the overtime
but most were just glad to work a regular ten-hour day,
have a couple of drinks and play with their kids. By then
he walked as if on a trampoline,
springing over the shoulders of the largest
men on earth. He was tattooed from the tips of his digits
through the vast ocean of his back and the wild
plains of his abdomen. These were brutal times, in a way,
the way cavemen were evolving and beating each other to death
with big rocks. The tribesmen sucking on the marrow
of a bone, etc. a whole course of sagging evolution happening.
My brother's ear lobes were giant horseshoes and his
pelvis held a mint of silver. His boots were made of
leopard fur and leopard leather and laced

together with the intestines of a giant. He was a sight in the
supermarket, eating a bag of onions while whiling his
way through the produce. His autograph was the size of
a guitar and his eyelids were like peach halves.
But that's all done with now, anyway. Long live the Captain
of Forever Suburbia! You would never get it, Tina. Never.

WAKE UP, TINA

I find the rain like a reminder of something, like,
I don't know, Holy Crap! It's Friday and in one room a child
is flushing a toilet and singing and in another room a
another is making lots of whooshing, zapping noises
and my dog is under my legs and my legs are up on the table
and someone says I'm looking down at the ceiling
and down there is danger that has the face of a, like,
deep down clown in a distance. Following the sound
of distances, yuck yuck yuck yuck yuck yuck!
Yuck yuck yuck yuck I say to my head because my head
needs a talking to. So I talk indeed as I cozy up
up with a blanket, a beanbag, and another blanket.
For some reason I get extra cold sometimes. Have you
experienced the sensation of being chilled? It's not like
you're freezing to death, but something unpleasant is happening.
I know long ago in different scenarios I imagined new ways
to cope with various sensations, but each time I have to
pull out the blanket I seem to lose a bit of my life.
It's hard to describe in detail, especially since you can
be such a little bitch! I'm trying to say something new
about the universe and all you care about is
padding your sense of security. Tina, you can be so petty!

A WARNING

Seriously, Tina, you know
what I mean because of
your years as a teacher.
I don't want to get into the details
in public, like this, all creepy
and whatnot. Trust me, you
don't want me to get into it.
Seriously, just let it go
and know that I could,
if I wanted to, devastate you!

HOW SOMETHING ISN'T NEW

I'm trying to grow into something
bloomy and pretty to the naked eye.
I want to be a bigger engine and to hum
louder than a novelist or a baker. I have daydreams
about what could happen, what might
manifest. In my chilled night hours, alone like
a wasp at a window, I buzz strongly and feel
likely to move into a new dormitory, where lunch
and dinner are served with dark bloody gravy. But
when nothing happens, I think of my children,
learning to be themselves and falling in love
with everything new. They are smart,
good kids. They make these high-pitched tiny
sounds with their mouths and laugh in bubbles.
They don't know the gravity that falls on the earth
or the lungs that power the body or the brains
which scramble the too-much info. They are
just blind moles of love who shuffle quietly around.
I think of birds sometimes.
Other times, without thinking it through, I notice
my surrounding and the terrible colors.
I feel spooky, Tina.
I feel deadly and flat.

PROFESSIONAL DEPRESSION

I want, I want, I want to be
something okay, with myself and the world!
O how I hate my longing! How I hate hating my world
and where it sits on me, with its heavy as hell
horse-faced world self, sitting on me and making me
barely breathe-y. There's hardly anything I'm capable of.
There's practically nothing in terms of hope
that I can weave through my very woolly hair.
I'm shit out of luck. Like you, fucker.
Go find some religion or something. Read some old
dude or some new dude and try to think squarely
about it. You're lost man. It's over. You can find
a map or an atlas or whatever, but there's no hope, man,
and no situation will fix it.

OBVIOUSNESS

One drives a car because the car is a set of functions that requires a person to activate them. So you activate that shit and you pull out of your driveway and you follow various signs and you direct your face and auto toward something that isn't immediately available. That is called the future. The future, as I understand it, is a concept meant to indicate something that may or may not happen in an hour that is to come. All of the hours that come seem similar to the hours that have passed, except for when they deviate wildly, causing very strange sensations that cause readjustments in the attitude or outlook of your mind-eye. Jesus, Tina, seriously, you should get this! All of your time studying various philosophy and yet you still look at me all gape-mouthed? It's simple: certain concepts instruct you pretty much just by thinking them!

EDDIE VAN HALEN

George Lynch is good, Tina,
and so are some other guys

but everyone knows that
Eddie Van Halen is the greatest

guitar player to ever live. I mean,
Hendrix and Clapton and Randy

Rhoads are fucking great and
they rock but Eddie Van Halen

was the only person in the world
who could play the solo on

Beat It. Also,
Eruption, Tina.

LOVING THE AFFECTED

I was standing there, like, no way! I'm not fucking kidding!
No way!
But there was another reality and that was a real deal happening
that was, like, not "no way," but, like, "yes, man, do it."
This terrible place in life that we move into, it's not ours for the taking,
rather, it's just ours.
Imagine the way police cars screech through traffic in a 1970s cop movie.
Imagine the reality television shows that show you humans who are worse
than yourself, Tina.
When you really consider the details, it's staggering. Or not. How do
you appreciate an older movie star actor or actress?
Do you like blue jeans and strut? Or satin and suave? It's not an
important question,
but not asking it would be a dereliction of duty. Course, there is
no duty, only empty fainting sounds.
The whole cast of faintees is semi-upset by their involvement, while
they understand there is no choice.
The ape in the circus is fake!
The cape and the top hat are fake!
Your little face, Tina, is beautiful!

THE BOXED

The stuff I've said could be stored in a jar and
jar after jar could line the pantry and each jar could
be stuffed full, with word after word. And the words
I haven't said could be stuffed in cans and canned
and frozen and put in the bottom of deep-freeze
refrigerators, or boxed in cardboard boxes and boxed
into a closet or left underneath some basement stairs.
The point is how impossible it is to say anything
worth listening to and how easy it is to try.
Many times, when I was a kid, I felt as if I couldn't
be heard and was rolled into a dough of silence.
My little robot ears heard failure in every sink of
drained water, in every jingle of the car keys,
in every dresser drawer opened. My, my ears were
alert! They were really jumpy! And now, all adultish
and brutal, I still hear my childhood in my whispers
to my children. I hear them walking about the house
and I feel lucky. I also feel stupid because I haven't made
sense of anything and here I am thinking.

FORM

What accrued over a number of days was a sort of structure,
a kind of architecture that shamed even some modern
engineers who couldn't envision just how something so disorganized
happened to jive in such a correct manner. But,
of course it accrued in this manner! WTF? Are you a dumbass?
Yes, the days and the eternally spinning mechanism
of O My Fucking God continue, and continue to accrue.
You can't possibly think you're special, right?

I just don't want to find myself in the scenario of having to comfort
you, ad nauseam, because, at some fucking party,
some dick, some whatever, made you question your identity.
My job, as I see it, is not to be a pillar you can lean on,
but to be a pillar you may or may not be able to count on.
It's a sort of Rube Goldberg device, a balancing act.
What, you think I make this shit up? Of course not!
I'm depending on you, too! We need each other, Tina!

MEETING ARRANGEMENTS

Arranging meetings is part of life and must
be attended to with the same diligence
applied to other aspects of life that are likewise
attended to. First, there must be a person elsewhere and
he or she will have to find a spot in the universe
coinciding with your spot in the universe,
and, at a specific hour, etc. In a perfectly namable
set of coordinates. How nice it is to have numbers! Or not, especially
when they mislead you
into thinking an equal sign that might not even be possible.
You have hopes!
You make phone calls!
You do this stuff in anticipation of something, Tina!
This isn't just good times until it becomes something more.
A whole lifetime happens and is gone, in a sad way,
out of the door over the dirt floor.
You are alone with memories and voices through
communication devices
and just a small, still drop of water falls through
your beard.
A tear in your beard is a very great country song.
Believe me, I'm open to certain possibilities!

IN A TRAFFIC JAM WITH TINA

I had decided that the dead deer didn't
have a penis. I stuck by this decision.
The dead deer had been ravaged
by, I assume, scavenging animals
like small mammals, birds, and rodents.
The deer was missing his knees,
I said.
And the deer was missing his stomach,
I said.
I said a lot of stuff. I was just answering
questions. It had been a long day.
So the deer is missing his hip
or his hoof, or whatnot. There is a very
bad decomposing deer smell.
I made the decision I made because
I had to. Some decision was necessary so,
I said,
the deer didn't have his penis.

TINA, BECAUSE I'M LAZY

I'm wasting my time. It's all I do, like I've got
an agenda and it's not there. I turn to this in an effort
to avoid that, and yet where I turn is into another
avenue that leads nowhere. It's like I waste time
in the same manner that time passes, identically,
as if my life and time were one and the same, and we
are skating on an ice of nothing, above a lake
of nothing, below a sky of nothing.
The things being wasted include the sound
of the ice skates, the long low rumble of the nonexistent
shaking lake, the whispery sound of our breath against
the unwindy wind. So I just keep going on and on,
wasting the wasting and wasting the wasting and
what else should I do? You got some big fucking idea?
I've got ideas too, but they're all wasted because that's
what all of them are about. You'd think I'd be smarter
than that, but I am. What I'm not is capable of being
myself. If I were, wow, would things change! I might
lift myself from this mess and move into your body
where I believe something is not wasted. Where, I think,
something really strange and bright is happening.

8:51 IN THE EVENING

I should work. I mean I need to get
some work done. There's work
I need to do, Tina. Like, I should do
that work that I've been meaning
to do. There's all this stuff that
I haven't done, that I need to do, so
I should do that shit and get it
over with. I need to work on
stuff that is related to my job. My
job is always requiring me to
work. I mean, seriously, it's always
saying (though of course it
isn't really a person and doesn't
actually say anything),
"Dude, get your shit
together. Do your work. Get
it done." And I say stuff like, "Yeah,
I know. I know. I know." I don't
know what to say to work. I mean,
I look at it. I think about it.
I know it has to get done and it
does get mostly done, but, then,
sometimes I guess it doesn't. I mean,
I know I should do it, but it's hard.
Why, is what I wonder. Why is
working on work so hard? I mean, it's

only work. Why should work be a
big deal? It shouldn't be. And yet,
every year my annual report
is due to my department and I think,
my god, you are simply work that
is unworkable. I cannot deal
with your inconvenient necessity.
I sit here thinking about the work.
Thinking about the work. Thinking,
what is work? What is work? Thinking
I've got to do work. I mean, I've just
got to do it.

CRIME, TINA

Being a criminal is situational. Either
the situation or the act happens or
other things may happen. It's often awfully
ambiguous. The situation or action is
often palpable but also possibly not
happening. What doesn't happen happens
often. Often, the non-happening is happening
so frequently that you can't even feel it.
That's when the law gets involved and
they start hassling or not hassling you,
or taking you into to custody or not, and,
my dear, there you stand as a regular asshole.
Not alone in the world, but not exactly as
part of a team. At those moments you freeze
into an idiot that nearly everyone knows. If
they don't know you, they think they do or
want to. It's all the same. Meanwhile,
a goofy quilt of sameness seems ill-formed
and loopy. Like stupid after-dinner mints
and other ideas that aren't good or bad all
on their own. I just make it up. Like you,
a poor imagination.

THE GOVERNMENT

The government isn't really fun.
At best, it's amusing, but fun wouldn't be the
first thought. I don't even have most thoughts,
or any. I just don't like the way it feels.
I also don't enjoy short term memory. Most
things feel funny, all clingy to my inner
Ferris wheel, all hickish, in cut-off jean shorts.
The whole problem with carney culture
can be summed up in one word. It's not an
obvious word, on the other hand, you don't
have to stretch too far to find it. When
things get bitter in my head, when the flag
of anxiety and sadness sails about
as a wizard's sleeve after certain spells,
then I get the impression that the government
isn't looking out for the funniest among us,
instead they'd like to push the funniest well-ward
and just let the firefighters and various
personnel try to extract them for days, all over
the media, etc. But they don't ever extract
them and so the funny stay dead there. And all
of these leads me back to the apostle Paul
and his quest to spread the gospel. Silly, gospel.
And then some dignified person would get up
on some sort of stage and say something graceful
and lay a wreath or something like that and
meanwhile, back at the ranch.

CRAZY

When it snows, the snowflakes just fall
out of the sky and every single one is identical.
That's the thing about snowflakes, no variation.
And the snow accumulating, like baked bread.
I've never understood why God hates yeast so much.
He's always, like, "make that bread unleavened, goddamnit!"
He just fucking hates the yeast. He likes
his bread flat and his meat burned. He likes the
pleasing aroma of a barbecue. There's so much I
don't understand. Like why it snows at all or why
there are seasons or why Gary Coleman had to die.
This stuff is never explained. Instead, we're expected
to just accept it, bury our heads in the identical
snowflakes and come home all frozey-headed. And
there are countries all around the world! And there
are people who are actors and people who are manual
laborers and other people who are other things!
It's fucking crazy! Meanwhile, a Saturday afternoon
happens and the snow just falls and falls and finally
lands, on earth, like everything else and just sits
there looking bland and stupid, like Tina.

SLEEPING IN A TREE WITH TINA

I haven't got much time to write this because I don't have much time, like everyone, who always says, "Hey, I'm everyone and I have so little time." I keep meaning to make more time in my basement. I have thought of baking my time, making it super fresh and breadish, so as to warm the house with the smell of a baked good, but I'm having trouble finding a good place to start. Last night, before bed, I could see the faces of my children and their faces did not look right, like maybe they weren't my children at all, just some kids who wandered in and got stuck. We all get stuck sometime. But really the important thing about words is that they exist. Remember how in high school certain words made everyone laugh? Remember how sexy sex was then? Remember how hard it was to remember to do what you knew you were supposed to do? Remember Algebra? Remember me, in my raincoat, coming to you with a sad glass of soda and a vague sense that the world was coming to an end? I can't remember anything anymore, only the outdoor world, before the discovery of fire, and how at night we'd just huddle up together and wait for it to pass.

AROUND THE AREA

The area around the area is the place
you're trying to find. You want to find this place,
lay down in it, rest your head or whatever
and then, man, you just deal with it.
This area, this placed area, is between the
verge and dirge of something else.
Many lonely people have witnessed and wrestled
with an extremely fast bluegrass song, so much
so that there's nothing left at all to hear, even
the fiddle player who rattles in a number of
different directions at once, even that sound
couldn't be emptier. My whole life, with
people around me, many of whom I love a lot
and some of whom I get very tired of, we are
like cabins in a forest, drifting through the woods
only because none of us are real. Dear red-headed
children, dear lost little robins, dear poor deers,
rabbits, strong avian types, and whiskery cats, please
hear these problems I am trying to pinpoint. You know,
consider yourself a fucking dobro if you have to,
but the point is that you elaborate toward
something very funky and right-thinking. It doesn't
matter to any of us if you live or die. That's
not really the issue. There's something more to
consider. Just understand what you're getting into,
Tina.

INSTRUCTIONS ON HOW TO PALPITATE BEST

The safest way is to
allow your heart (or other
palpitation device) to
palpitate in its normal
way. Do not interfere
with palpitating. Do not
apply electric shocks unless
trained in applying electric
shocks. Do not massage
in palm of hand unless
trained in palpitation hand
massage. I hate that
I have to tell you these
things, Tina, but it's
important. Do allow
research to continue,
Tina. Don't get in
the way of progress.

SO LONG

This nonsense about the applesauce
and all that horseshit about the petitions
and all that crap about the articles
in the brochure and then there was all that talk
about the birthday, and how what's-his-face
screwed you over when it came to the bake sale,
and, in all seriousness, I hardly know
what to say. Tina, you're a terrible person.
I've spent years justifying your insecurities
and your violent displays of power, but, listen, I've
grown up, man, I'm not that kid I used to be. There's
no way I'm going to change the program at this point.
I know it's killing you, but I'm not changing the
backdrop or the postcards. You can have the stuff
in the fridge and you're welcome to remove all
of the samples you provided, but, beyond that,
it's over. No more late nights at the lake, no more
Sunday gifts and calls from the highway. I'm not going
to remove the tags anymore or spray the apartment.
As far as I know, everyone else feels
the same way. You can ask, but I don't know.
Whatever. Whatever. You say you have my best interests
at heart, but the a evidence is a touch bleaker.
I don't know. I don't know anymore. It's just
lonely now is all I'm saying. Jesus, Tina, try to step
outside of yourself for a moment or two! You've

got to make changes! You've got to give up the Nazi shit. You've got to change your hairstyle. You've got to move on, Tina. You're dragging us around like a dead clown! It's time to let childish things go!

MOTHER'S DAY

I feel my best when I'm on a skateboard.
On a skateboard,
I am another human, one more mobile
and more attached to a small plank of wood
set atop four small wheels.
My wife is very beautiful, Tina.
Physically it's like she is trying to eclipse
her inner goodness.
It's like she has decided to grow
a force field around her inner goodness
by creating a shell of beauty
that no one would dare penetrate. I have
penetrated this shell and am lucky.
Tina, I have been lucky
to be inside my wife
and watch my kids expand her belly
and see her explode with them.
She is not a skateboard but I am
free when I am sailing on her.
I look at her and the sea waits.
My ollie, sometimes, is
perfect, Tina. When it is, she snaps into the air
and when I land
my feet are just glued.

HAVING REAL IDEAS

No one cares if this is written or if I say
something or nothing. No one cares if, for once,
something happens or doesn't. I know people
who have strong feelings, but very few
of them know my initials. I have parents but
they have no bullhorns or cheer routines. No
one cares if I move on to something else, or if I stick
to something for a long, long, lengthy time.
Time gets very stretchy, very warmish taffy.
Time possess a similarity in sweetness and plasticity.
Also, there are wars and rumors of wars.
Also, for God so loved his something.
Also, there are different allusions that could be created
and many of them could be biblical in nature.
For instance, well, I think this has been covered.
For instance, fear not, for thou are with me, be
very afraid because I'm not easy to find but
I'm watching from a vase of fake flowers, Tina!

THE SPIRIT WORLD

What else in this universe but
a disco ball of doom and a DJ,
Tina, who won't play the song you
want, but won't quit playing
all the other songs? That DJ is
DJ GOD MUTHA FUCKA
and he can rock your shit for
a while, but, eventually, he's
going to leave you and you're
not going to get a chance to
say goodbye, Tina, and, when
you get home, that night, you're
gonna cry, cry, cry because you're
his silly little bitch.

ACCORDING TO ALL THE DEAD PEOPLE

According to all the dead people, death
is a pretty silent place, where people don't
make any attempts at communication or
whatnot, movement. Of course, I know people
believe in ghosts, but I don't buy it.
I mean when the Bible discusses all
of the exceptions to death, it never mentions
handball or windsurfing.
I'm thinking, WTF, Bible, you're not even
including these very minor sports? How can
I expect you to help me when all
you want to discuss is God and his
goofy preferences regarding culinary
issues? I wouldn't think he'd care about food
at all. But, he does. And apparently it's a big
deal to him, Tina. In fact, he so concerned
about the situation of yeast in bread
that he can't even think straight!

ONE PROBLEM WITH CHILDREN

Tina, the only known solution to a lost child is to
find the child and return the child to wherever
the child is from. There's a girl lost in the neighborhood.
There are children all over the world who disappear.
There are children everywhere who are being mistreated
badly. So much so that nobody understands the
nature of, say, even a basketball game. We look like
very stupid faces when we get on TV and try to
predict the course of the future. O, the future! That
vibrant little package of hope! We are unwrapping
it even now. Even now we are unwrapping it more.
It keeps unwrapping and we keep speaking about
our faces and how stupid they are. Even very stupid
writing poetry! I mean, of course, your precious poetry.
The parts you don't count on are what sticks from the past,
that violent mercurial beast of Cling Town. From those
cages whole hosts are unleashed and breathe forth
with biblical happiness. Which is hardly happy but
at least able to set fire to cities and kill, say, everything.

REALER

I don't believe in ghosts, Tina. Meaning,
I don't believe that spirits live on or something
and then kinda float around knocking things over
and causing water pipes to make extra noises
and/or maybe making semi-scary moaning
sounds and/or appearing as bright orbs or
something in the background or foreground
of photographs. I know people say they've
seen ghosts and heard ghosts and felt
ghostly presences and all of that, but I don't
buy it. I think all of those people are in some way
mistaken. I don't think they're lying, I just think
they're confused about what happened. Have you
been confused before? It's an unpleasant sensation.
To remedy this sensation, human beings come
up with explanations. These explanations vary
in their degree of believability. I myself have
believed stuff before. That sensation is much
more enjoyable than the sensation of confusion.
Confusion feels funny in your bones, Tina. It might
shift around a little and make you feel as if you're
on a boat. That boat may be in a storm. That
storm may be causing giant waves to crash on
the deck. That deck needed to be cleaned anyway.
The death of the sailors is like the death of all
ghosts, sinking to the floor of the ocean and waiting
there, patiently, for something to make them realer.

THE RESCUE OPERATION

I keep thinking of the beasts
in the field and the soil in the earth.
I also think of the yolk in the egg
and the egg in the belly of the alligator. I can
imagine the air lifting the leaves and the
trees teeming with certain grubs. I keep
thinking of the shellfish in the sea
and the water that it takes to move
a large, large ship through the ocean. I am
barely thinking of Tina now. Barely
imagining how she forms words with her
mouth and with the words she forms
whole rotations and spins. Sometime,
in the dark volcano of clocks, something will
rise up and up and, like a bird or a
paper airplane, sail out of this joint, into
the box where the rest of us are just waiting
with our tied, tiny hands and our gags.

HURTS

There is an action in the world referred to as
suicide and people take this action from time
to time and they leave behind friends and family
and loved ones and then those
people live with the loss of the person who used
the suicide action to leave this place for something
better. I don't mean for heaven, or nirvana, or
some sort of beach resort where there is always
an open bar and open buffet and parrots saying
words and beautiful people walking around in
angelic bathing suits. The something better they
are after is simply something not here, and so
they go, to see what is not here. And what they leave
behind is what is not here, anymore. They leave
this space that was once full of humanness but is
now full of a complete unfullness. And we, the people
looking at this unfullness, feel anxious and scared
because it was all so simple and so easy to accomplish.
To watch the world drain and become empty is easy.
There is suddenly more air everywhere. Everywhere
you look all you see is more air. And air is a good thing
but more air is scary and so you try to breathe it
all in as quickly as possible. There is this idea that you
can convert it to life. And you can. It just hurts.

THE SITUATION OFTEN REFERRED TO AS POETRY

There is a situation often referred to as poetry. If you don't
understand that, we're at an impasse. Other situations are
possible, including stock car racing, but most of these
events go undetected. It's similar to alien life forms or
endless rope tricks. Even special cowboys can't lasso
every single lamb in the universe. Even house cats
look stupid in the bathroom mirror. For me, and my family,
we have numerous sweatshirts and various family traditions.
One of these is to exhaust ourselves in our sleep so
that when we awake we are livelier and smarter because
we're so tired. At other times, we dress ourselves in robes
and lounge about the house, whistling softly and jutting
our bellybuttons toward the ceiling. My wife will
bring me ideas about capitalism or whatnot, perhaps
a recipe for veggie burgers. The thought of it all makes
me jumpy with love. The poetry we read to each other
makes us giggle. It's always stuff like "you have a
ginormous, orange band-aid on" and other things like that
that just make you go, whoa.

I SAID GOODBYE

It was easy, Tina. I just said it.
It rolled off my wedge-like tongue
like nothing. I didn't even
feel it. It was probably
easier than this is making
it seem. It was easy. I said,
"Goodbye." And like that—nothing flashed,
nothing moved, nothing changed,
nothing noticed. Not even me.
I didn't even notice it. I just
said it. It was quick too. Like
a sixteenth the length
of saying, "Goodbye." When
I was gone nothing was questioned
or re-evaluated. It's only now that
I'm revisiting it. And now?
Nothing. I can't feel
anything inside me, Tina.
Not a whimper or mummer.
Not the sound of water
slushing in your belly,
or your kid's belly. There
wasn't even *that* sound.

THE EGYPTIAN REVOLUTION OF 2011

I just love my kids. I mean what does love even mean
when you've got my kids involved. I'm so glad when it's
a snow day and they get to stay home from school. I think
it's fucking great when there's a snow day. I think it's great
when they're home. And in this moment when they're
not here and I'm alone in this house I start writing
and what do I start writing I start writing how
I love my kids. I am amazed at myself, really. I mean what
can I do, as a human? I can love my kids a shit ton is one
thing. I didn't know I could be so loving. I never figured
I was unloving, I just didn't know I'd love my kids so much.
I really love them. It is icy out but I took them each
to a friend's house for something to do. I want them to
be happy, happy, happy, happy, happy, happy.
I hope they grow into large machines of love who swell around
town and make little quiet neighborhoods weep. I hope
they have kids so I can have kids again who maybe I will
love like how I love my kids. Maybe they'll be like my kids
and so I will love them how I love my kids.
What I love about my kids is unbelievable. I don't believe it.
It's such a world of love that there is no word for it.
And what really kills me is that many other people in this
world, who are humans, have felt the love that I have for my
kids and their love is no different and my love is no better
and my love in no more pure or less pure or unequal to
in any way. This is nothing to mention, how much I love

my kids. There is nothing to say about that at all. This
dangerous fucking world with its corruptness
and violent revolutions and whatnot. Bull whips and
slip knots and ugly ugly messy stuff. And it's only
so ugly and ugly and messy and stuff because of how much
I love my kids.

ACKNOWLEDGMENTS

Thanks to Shanna Compton, Matt Hart, Tom Koontz, Max Greenstreet, Jennifer L. Knox, Flipper Eight, Veronica Saltwater and, as always, Kitty.

Thanks to the editors of the following journals, who published some of these poems: *Atticus Review,* the *Bakery, Country Music, Court Green, Everyday Genius,* the *Good Men Project, interrupture, Lamination Colony, MiPOesias, Spooky Boyfriend,* and *Stoked.*

Design: Shanna Compton • Cover photo: Lost & Taken

ABOUT THE AUTHOR

Peter Davis lives with his sweet wife, son and daughter. His poems have appeared in places like *Atticus, Jacket,* and the *Best American Poetry* anthology. He draws, writes and makes music in Muncie, Indiana while teaching English at Ball State University. More info at artisnecessary.com.

PRAISE FOR *TINA* & PETER DAVIS

Warning: If you're looking to find out who Tina is, these poems won't help you very much. But if you're interested in reading the work of one of our most obsessively inventive, hilariously human, and sometimes crushingly affecting poets, then you've come to the right book. Through a series of direct addresses and lyric effusions to "Tina," Peter Davis reminds us that sometimes talking, even casually, to anyone else is always talking significantly to oneself—and by extension, all of us. *TINA* is a suckerpunch, and then you see stars. Sometimes it's so funny, it hurts a little bit, and sometimes it hurts so much, it just hurts. —**Matt Hart**

Peter Davis is considered to be one of the most important American contemporary poets. —*Time Out Tel Aviv*

The consistent, unabashed persona that Davis writes in creates a rhythm that often echoes the pace of the reader's thoughts—it is fluid, sometimes quick, and difficult to control. Davis builds a platform for our imaginations to fill in the blank. —*H_NGM_N,* **Curtis Purdue**

Davis works in the same vein as John Ashbery, by making things so personal, they're universal.
—*The Best American Poetry,* **Michael Schiavo**

Peter Davis is a master of the prose poem format.
—*Midwest Book Review*

Poems that shriek with personality, honesty and humor and goodness.
—*Vouched Books*

In an environment in which so many seem to steer their sculls between appointed lines, Peter Davis's poems motorboat back and forth across poetry currents—satirically, yes, but also intelligently, self-aware, and shrewdly critical. Davis's brilliantly bizarre [first] book both parodies and plays homage to precursors as varied as Frank O'Hara, Robert Bly, and Russell Edson; tests the limits of traditional form; and isn't afraid to act unassumingly goofy, putting, in the words of Amy Gerstler, 'the id through a juicer.' His new work tackles assumptions not of the canon, but of the writing process itself. The awkwardly plain, self-conscious tone is both startlingly ironic and subtly perceptive. Peter's poems make me laugh aloud or shake my head, wondering how and where he unearths their chutzpah! —*The Best American Poetry,* Bruce Covey

Peter Davis has already established himself as an innovator with a great deal of intelligence and skill. Modest but assured, he explores ideas most poets would not think to broach and pushes the accepted limits of form in ways that expand what a poem can be. Davis knows that in order to break ground a writer must be bold and open to uncertainties. Davis's sense of play services a unique moral vision. –*HTMLGiant,* Tony Leuzzi

Davis is a writer who captures the reader's attention immediately with a candor uncommon in contemporary poetry. [He] has reimagined the persona poem, as practiced by Rilke, John Berryman and others. Contemporary poetry has often been attacked for abandoning the public. Davis embraces the public without any loss of sophistication. His work is direct, frank, refreshing, thoughtful and funny.

—*Escape Into Life,* Mark Kerstetter

www.ingramcontent.com/pod-product-compliance
Lightning Source LLC
Chambersburg PA
CBHW032132090426
42743CB00007B/575